FLOWERS
IN THE
GARDEN

F

FRANCES LINCOLN LIMITED
PUBLISHERS

FLOWERS IN THE GARDEN

ANDI CLEVELY

PHOTOGRAPHS BY
STEVEN WOOSTER

Frances Lincoln Ltd
4 Torriano Mews
Torriano Avenue
London NW5 2RZ
www.franceslincoln.com

Infinite variety is the key to
the success with which
flowering plants have settled
and colonized almost every
kind of habitat a garden can
offer, whether hot and dry
(page 1), waterlogged (page
2) or dappled sunlight in the
shade of trees (right).

CONTENTS

INTRODUCTION

Flowers like rose-pink delphiniums, hybrid hellebores and the dazzling range of modern double fuchsias have come a long way since their simple ancestors first appeared on Earth millions of years ago. But although archaeological finds suggest that flowers have been cultivated and appreciated since well before earliest records, the enormous profusion and variety that we take for granted today is a phenomenon of very recent centuries.

A flower border (pages 6–7) can be a celebration of diversity, matching or contrasting flowers with appealing colours, heights and shapes to create an apparently natural work of beauty.

Possibly the simplest and most widespread flower type, daisies such as feverfew (*Tanacetum parthenium*, left) have been popular for centuries, bringing a natural careless charm to any garden style.

species growing in the surrounding countryside.

The Victorians were the first to make colourful and adventurous gardening fashionable, and it was their extraordinary appetite for novelties that provided the main stimulus for breeding new flowers. The advent of popular gardening magazines helped spread this passion to all social classes, encouraging trend-setting styles such as carpet bedding and the herbaceous border as well as specialist-interest societies like the working-class florist clubs, which focused on breeding and exhibiting flowers such as show auriculas, carnations, laced pinks and tulips.

Developing new varieties relied then mainly on selecting, isolating and refining superior flower forms and chance mutations or 'sports' until they grew true to type as distinctly original cultivars. Deliberate scientific breeding only became widespread in the latter part of the nineteenth century, and has evolved since into the highly organized and competitive industry behind the glamorous seed and plant catalogues that beguile us annually with the latest crop of new flower varieties and improved strains.

In Shakespeare's time choice of flowers was limited to a very small selection of ancient favourites, wildflowers and medicinal plants. Great collectors like the Tradescants were discovering new flowers in the sixteenth century, but these introductions were often delicate or expensive exotics intended to grace the idealized landscapes and lavish glasshouses of grand estates. The ordinary gardener had the time, energy and ability to grow only food plants and a few 'cottage garden' flowers, which were often little different from native

The most successful summer bedding plants, such as pelargoniums, fuchsias and lobelias, are a triumph of the flower breeder's art, supplying lasting colour and interest for a variety of situations.

FLOWERS FOR ALL

Everyone can – and arguably should – grow flowers. Very often it takes only an inexpensive packet of seeds to produce a multitude of vigorous plants whose sole aim in life is to bear flowers. With the vast assortment available of unsophisticated or fleeting annuals, tender bedding varieties for summer exuberance, and robust perennials that fatten and bloom more profusely as the years pass, it is not difficult to fill a garden with glorious colour, form and fragrance.

Do not grow so many that you overlook the singular beauty and detail of individual blooms, though – the teardrops which appear each morning in the drooping flowers of crown imperials (*Fritillaria imperialis*), for example, said to be their response to a rebuke from the gods intended to teach the proudest flower in the Garden of Eden a due sense of humility. Watch morning glories unfurl their heavenly blue trumpets with breathtaking speed when the early sunshine first strikes their fresh buds, or pause a little longer to follow lesser celandine flowers as they rotate and track the sun's path across the sky. Gently brush primrose or dianthus flowers and let yourself be carried away by their seductive perfume.

Apart from these hedonistic pleasures and the sense of vitality and closeness to nature that plants introduce into a domestic setting, there are important environmental benefits attached to growing flowers. Many are a crucial food source for various kinds of wildlife, sometimes one that helps ensure their survival: only bumble bees can extract the nectar secreted in the typical hood of an aconitum (monkshood) flower, for example. This relationship is mutual, because the monkshood relies on the foraging bee to incidentally fertilize its blooms: as a result the wild plants' range is confined to that of its pollinators. Insects like hoverflies and lacewings – allies in gardeners' attempts to control plant pests – favour gardens where there are plenty of the flowers they like to browse, fertilizing them as they go.

Growing your own flowers to gather for vases and arrangements can indirectly assist the environment because the worldwide commercial cut-flower industry is one of the heaviest consumers of artificial fertilizers, chemical pesticides and air transport.

The precise and eventual effects of global climate change are still uncertain, but there is already menacing evidence of unbearable pressures on plants growing in habitats that are being stressed beyond tolerance thresholds. These threats to wild species, combined with the steady loss of old flower varieties in favour of the new, suggest that gardens might become vital sanctuaries for a range of endangered plants.

THE IMPORTANCE OF BEING PARTICULAR

The challenge for many people is not so much finding reasons to grow flowers or collecting enough to populate the garden, but quite the contrary: the temptation to include something of everything can be so irresistible that practical constraints are easily overlooked.

It is not enough to like the look of a flower. Buying any plant on impulse without considering where it is to live can result in failure: if it doesn't like its new home, it won't grow. At best it could turn out to be a disappointment. The fantastically multi-coloured *Houttuynia cordata* 'Chameleon', for example, loses all its startling tints and becomes a dull blueish-green in shade; bluebells survive but often refuse to flower without plenty of sunshine in early spring; and nominally hardy fuchsias can die right back where temperatures fall much below –5C (22°F).

Every plant species, from chickweed to the most magnificent orchid, is the result of adaptation over countless generations to a particular set of living conditions – a specific kind of soil, level of drainage, average temperature range, exposure to light and so on. For the greatest chance of success and satisfaction with a new plant, you need to take these preferences into account and try to arrange a place in the garden that closely resembles its original habitat.

Read on to explore the remarkable world of flowers and discover the essential stages of selecting the best varieties to match your plans. However exacting your criteria might be, there will still be plenty to choose from.

Every flower has evolved to fit a particular set of environmental demands – hence their different shapes and structures, all designed to attract pollinators. Gardeners, however, usually mix or partner them according to colour and flowering season.

Defining terms

Several different plant types are grown in gardens for their flowers. For practical purposes they may be divided into two. Woody kinds are trees, shrubs and many climbers with permanent stems that do not usually die down in winter. Herbaceous plants are distinguished by the production of new, soft topgrowth each year of their life expectancy, which may be annual, biennial or perennial (see page 22), and are what is generally understood by the expression 'garden flowers'. These herbaceous flowering plants are the subject of this book.

1

The WORLD of FLOWERS

Flowers grow wherever there is a suitable place for them to put down roots. Infinitely varied in appearance and character, they offer a host of tantalizing possibilities for gardeners to investigate when in search of perfect plants to fill beds, borders and containers with colour, life and beauty. Their almost dazzling diversity, however, is the result of long adaptation to local, sometimes very demanding conditions, and understanding their individual qualities and requirements is the key to identifying the best kinds for every garden purpose.

HOW FLOWERS BEGAN

The evolution and development of flowering plants is a fascinating tale of sex and exploitation.

Plants were around long before the first real flower opened on the prehistoric world. Although primitive, these early kinds, some of which are still around today, were already miracles of organization and complexity.

They had developed chlorophyll, the unique green leaf pigment that distinguishes plants from animals and allows them to produce energy from sunlight in the vital process called photosynthesis. Without this animals (including humanity) could not survive, because we are what we eat.

Plants had managed to emerge from the sea and colonize dry land, exchanging a drifting existence in water for a settled life, safely rooted in one place where they were exposed to more sunlight.

Size increased. Primitive land plants were small and simple, and required moisture for male reproductive cells to swim around and find females; later kinds like horsetails and ferns evolved spores that are more independent of moisture, allowing taller plants to multiply and move further inland.

A huge evolutionary leap was the appearance of seeds. Taller plants and trees like conifers and ginkgos lifted their heads into the wind, which carried male pollen and fertile seeds from place to place.

Explore the varied world of flowers for the perfect match between plant and place: lupins will jostle sociably as a mass landscape feature (page 12), for example, whereas the singular detail and simplicity of many clematis (left) deserve solo prominence.

The importance of sex

Early plants multiplied by splitting into daughters that were almost always the same as their parents (in the same way, gardeners divide, layer or take cuttings to propagate identical young plants). Only chance mutation produced new variants. Sexual reproduction allowed male and female to merge their characteristics in a host of novel combinations: just ten plants could produce over 59,000 variants very quickly. Breeding new flower varieties today still relies on this evolutionary breakthrough.

These early antecedents give no obvious hint of the next stage, the arrival of flowering plants. No one knows where or how they developed, and Charles Darwin called their abrupt appearance on the scene 100 million years ago 'an abominable mystery'. But the evolution of flowers is regarded as the apex of plant development as well as making possible the glory of gardens everywhere.

WHAT IS A FLOWER?

With very few exceptions – such as the dried tumbleweed that breaks free and rolls in the wind over North American prairies every autumn – plants are rooted to the spot and unable to move further than their stems can reach.

It was the emergence of flowers that permitted plants in different places to cross-pollinate and produce seeds that might be spread far afield to new sites. To do this efficiently a plant needs the help of an agent such as wind, animals or an insect, and the successful development of flowers depended on exploiting these intermediaries.

Any flower is essentially a highly specialized fertile shoot that produces pollen and often nectar or fragrance, with its leaves modified into petals in a multitude of colours, shapes and patterns. At its heart is a structure of male and female organs (occasionally these occur on separate flowers or plants), and an ovary in which the seeds form

Close study of any flower reveals a miracle of evolutionary perfection – an apparently artless and flamboyant poppy bloom, for example, is at heart an ingenious and streamlined reproductive mechanism.

and ripen. However gardeners assess and value flowers, their prime function is successful reproduction.

The qualities of different flowers co-evolved according to which particular agent that was best at pollinating it or dispersing its seed. For example, many green flowers rely on the wind and have no need to advertise themselves to other agents with bright colours, sweet nectar or alluring scent. Red or yellow flowers are pollinated in some parts of the world by birds, which can see these shades of the colour spectrum very well. Heavily perfumed, night-flowering plants often depend on bats to fertilize them, while many tubular blooms co-evolved with a particular long-beaked bird or insects with long tongues.

To see these partnerships in action, watch flies browsing the accessible upturned flowers of various daisies, a hummingbird hawk moth sipping nectar from the long spur at the back of an impatiens (busy Lizzie) flower, or bumble bees rummaging in the deep recesses of some flowers with their long tongues while their body hairs pick up pollen for transfer elsewhere.

Gardeners can exploit these mutual arrangements by

Crown imperials (*Fritillaria imperialis*) need to work hard in spring if they are to complete their growth cycle before emerging tree canopies block their supply of sunlight; after flowering and setting seed, they can then settle into the shade and gently retreat back to dormancy below ground.

planting appropriate flowers to encourage useful or attractive insects into the garden. Good butterfly flowers include catmint, golden rod, honesty, hyssop, Michaelmas daisies, petunias, pinks, scabious and stocks. For bees grow alyssum, bluebells, godetia, foxgloves, lupins, nasturtiums and sea lavender.

A HIDDEN AGENDA

With their numerous, often ingenious ways of organizing seed production and widespread dispersal, flowers diversified rapidly into a vast range of different types that went on to colonize almost every part of the Earth's surface.

Each of these types has a unique personality, in most cases a subtle combination of nature and nurture. First there is its appearance, its distinctive colour, shape, texture, size and all the other obvious qualities, which usually explain its appeal to gardeners and the reason for choosing to grow it in the garden.

But like every other species in existence it also has hidden characteristics that developed and were refined over generations of ancestors, and which fitted it for survival in the particular surroundings where it first settled and grew. Gardeners often take it for granted that any flower that catches their fancy can be planted in the garden and, with a little basic care, should flourish there. They often blame failure on poor cultivation or some other cultural factor, but the real reason often lies elsewhere, deep in its genetic make-up.

LIFESTYLE

A distinctive feature of a modern garden is that it usually hosts a cosmopolitan collection of plants from all over the world, from a variety of countries, climates and habitats, each with a different set of local conditions to which native plants had to adjust. If they didn't, they simply died out. In a garden the outcome will be similarly disappointing if a plant's capabilities and requirements do not match the growing environment it is given, and choosing the best kind to grow depends as much on recognizing its constitutional fitness as on the obvious appeal of its flowers.

Many characteristics of a plant can be explained by adaptation: the way it has successfully solved the problems and pressures of existence in its native habitat. Alpines, for example, are often low and compact, and sometimes an almost stemless mound or cushion of tiny leaves, enabling them to evade wind damage and

Rodgersias and candelabra primulas might almost have evolved as perfect wetland partners, the handsome foliage plant capturing maximum light in moist shade with its extravagant leaves, above which the tall blooms of primula spires reach up for a place in the sun, conspicuous to pollinating insects.

withstand drought during prolonged freezing. Tough plants adapted to the harshest climate, they can rot or refuse to flower if grown in wet, warm conditions.

Succulents like sedums and sempervivums tolerate extreme heat and drought because their fleshy foliage has become an emergency water store, while their leaf shapes (spheres, cylinders or compressed rosettes) restrict their surface area and so resist drying out. These, too, can rot in prolonged damp or heavy shade.

Climbers such as clematis or sweet peas enjoy the cool moist root run normally found in shady woodland, but have sacrificed bulk in favour of tall, slim twining or clinging stems that hitch a ride up other plants to hoist their flowers into sunlight.

Day length often affects flowering season. Woodland plants like primroses and bluebells bloom in the spring sunshine while trees are still bare and light levels high. Many summer bedding plants, on the other hand, come from tropical regions where seasonal change is less dramatic or non-existent, and their flowering is controlled more by their age, the ambient temperatures and light levels.

Appreciating these peculiarities helps when selecting flowers for particular aspects (sun or shade, for example), microclimates (wet or drought-prone sites) or seasonal displays, such as spring bedding and winter containers. There is a range of suitable candidates for every position and purpose, as chapter 2 reveals.

Even a cursory survey of the plant kingdom reveals dramatic contrasts in flower shapes and adaptations, from the demure pendent bells of Solomon's seal (opposite) and jaunty spikes of yellow loosestrife (top right) to the neatly tufted topknot of a typical thistle (bottom right), a model of economy for tough spartan sites.

FAMILY CONNECTIONS

Botanists attempt to understand and explain the huge numbers and diversity of plants by classifying them in groups according to their apparent evolutionary age – magnolias and buttercups are among the oldest, orchids and sunflowers the most recent on the scene. Flowers that exhibit similar physical features are assumed to be related (even though superficially they may look quite different), which can be very baffling. No gardener, for example, could confuse cyclamen with primroses (*Primula vulgaris*), tiny creeping Jenny (*Lysimachia nummularia*) or tall yellow loosestrife (*Lysimachia vulgaris*), but because their flowers have the same number of individual parts they are all grouped together as relatives in the primrose family (the *Primulaceae*).

PRACTICAL FLOWER GROUPS

Familiarity with botanical names helps us understand a plant's uniqueness and ancestry, and can sometimes be

21

a clue to its behaviour: the specific *aestivus* means 'summer-flowering', for example, *arboreus* is 'like a tree', *fruticosa* equals 'bushy', *sempervirens* 'evergreen'.

A Latin name does not teach us much else about how or where to grow it, however, and gardeners tend to use more prosaic groupings like 'annuals', 'bulbs', 'acid-loving' or 'climbers', which can immediately suggest the appropriate role for a plant in the garden.

HOW LONG IS A LIFETIME?

The commonest flower classification is based on lifespan. Botanically a lifetime is a very rough and ready, sometimes meaningless measurement. Primitive plants like plankton live for a few days, even hours, whereas the most ancient trees are several thousand years old. A single wild blackberry can root itself and spread for centuries over an indefinite distance, while lilies may fade away after a few years from declining vigour, starvation or simple wear and tear, rather than genuine old age.

For practical purposes, however, most gardeners simply divide flowering plants into annuals (lasting for a year), biennials (taking two years to bloom before dying) and perennials, which flower year after year.

Annuals have short busy lives in which they must pack maximum flower and seed production. This survival strategy makes subjects like tobacco plants (left) and nasturtiums (right) justly popular choices for summer colour in gardens.

ANNUALS

An annual flower is nominally one that grows from seed germination to seed dispersal in a year. Popular examples include clarkia, love-in-a-mist (*Nigella damascena*), nasturtiums and sweet peas.

Frost-tolerant annuals such as pot marigolds (*Calendula officinalis*), godetia, larkspur and annual cornflowers (*Centaurea cyanus*) are known as hardy annuals (abbreviated to HA) or winter annuals, because they may be sown or will self-seed to come up in early autumn and bloom the following summer, often living in reality for fourteen or fifteen months. Otherwise they are sown in spring to flower as smaller plants three to four weeks later than those over-wintered.

Many common weeds are hardy annuals, swiftly carpeting bare ground or disturbed soil and seeding after only a few weeks: groundsel and chickweed, for example, can take just six weeks to grow and shed many thousand seeds per plant. They are sometimes called ephemerals because they complete their lifecycle so quickly that they can manage several fleeting generations in a single season, which explains their notorious success and persistence in gardens.

Species whose seeds are too tender to withstand the rigours of winter are called summer or half-hardy annuals (HHA) and are sown in spring or early summer to germinate when frost is no longer a danger. They include felicia, morning glory (*Ipomoea*), tobacco plant (*Nicotiana*) and sunflowers. Many familiar summer bedding and container plants like lobelia, petunias, impatiens and coleus (*Solenostemon*) are strictly tender perennials that are usually grown from seed in the same way as half-hardy annuals and started early in artificial heat.

Although some sophisticated gardeners are derogatory about annuals, dismissing them as slightly uncouth or 'weedy' plants, deficient in quality and substance or demanding more care than their short season of naive or gaudy flowers deserves, most species are in fact singularly beautiful, with a typically airy and casual grace. They are usually very easy to grow and indispensable for a number of special roles in the garden as well as making excellent cut flowers. And far from being unrefined, annuals are regarded in evolutionary terms as the most advanced and specialized herbaceous plants, equipped to survive the most extreme conditions simply and efficiently as dormant seeds.

BIENNIALS

These flower, set seed and die in the second season after germination. Like annuals they tend to come from unstable or unpredictable habitats where fast growth is a virtue and short lifespan a means of diverting energy into producing as many seeds as possible before dying.

By postponing flowering until the second year, biennials are generally able to make more substantial plants than annuals, and are poised to bloom soon after reviving from winter dormancy. Many come from regions with short growing seasons or from woodland surroundings where delaying flowering until early the following season is a sound survival strategy. This biennial habit makes plants like wallflowers and Brompton stocks ideal candidates for spring bedding displays.

Many hardy biennials (HB) pass the winter unscathed as a weatherproof rosette of leaves or a buried fleshy root (a number of important vegetables like cabbages and parsnips are in fact the energy-rich winter storage phase of biennial plants). True biennials like Canterbury bells (*Campanula medium*) or some foxgloves then reawaken and produce one or more flowering stems, a relatively short flush of sometimes spectacular blooms, and a lavish crop of seeds that ripen in time to fall and grow into full-size plants before winter.

A number of popular 'biennials', such as sweet Williams, *Bellis perennis*, winter pansies and wallflowers,

Although usually grown as a self-seeding biennial, the common foxglove (distinguished from more complex hybrids by their one-sided flower spikes) may survive as a short-lived perennial, especially in its favourite slightly acid woodland shade, where its sideshoots often produce a second flush of bloom in early autumn.

Monocarpic plants

This means 'once-fruiting' and so describes plants that die after flowering and setting seed. It could accurately apply to annuals and true biennials, but usually refers to plants taking more than two years to flower. Examples include several kinds of Asiatic and blue poppies (*Meconopsis*), some alpine saxifrages and sempervivums, and *Agave americana,* the renowned 'century plant', which often takes fifty years or more to bloom. Many monocarpic species produce daughter plants (offsets) or suckers as well as seeds before dying. Occasionally bulbs like cardiocrinums seem to vanish after flowering and might be thought monocarpic, but they are usually found to have split into numerous bulblets which then need several years to reach flowering size.

Fleeting but irresistible poppies from the Himalayan hills, blue meconopsis species are typically monocarpic or short-lived perennials in gardens, especially on dry soils, but often self-seed freely in the moist, slightly acid and humus-rich conditions where they are most at home.

are truly perennial in ideal conditions, but in many gardens either succumb from over-indulgence – wallflowers prefer a frugal life in stony, well-drained surroundings – or are discarded after flowering to make room for the next display. Some can be perpetuated from year to year by standard perennial propagation techniques such as division or cuttings (see pages 81–7).

PERENNIALS

These are plants that live for several years and flower annually once mature. The group strictly includes trees, shrubs and other woody-stemmed plants, but most gardeners use the expression to mean border or herbaceous perennials: plants which produce new fleshy stems each spring and then die down to pass the winter resting as a dormant crown or clump of barely active roots. (There are exceptions such as oriental poppies, which rest after flowering in early summer until new foliage appears in the autumn).

Some border perennials, such as bergenias, dianthus, heuchera and tiarella, are evergreen or semi-evergreen, keeping all or most of their foliage during the winter months and so maintaining an often welcome visible green presence throughout the year in all but the coldest gardens.

The majority of popular kinds are hardy perennials (HP), but some have only borderline tolerance of frost, and in

Hardy perennials are perfect companions in a rose garden, their routine care causing minimal disturbance to the roses' roots. Here cream astilbes provide a long season of ferny foliage and airy plumes of flowers that can be left for autumn interest after they fade.

First-year flowers

Most perennials are added to the garden as growing plants, particularly if a named form is wanted, but some species or varieties can be grown from seed (see page 92) with fairly predictable and consistent results. If sown under cover in early spring the following kinds should start flowering in their first year:

- *Achillea* Summer Pastels Group,
- *Agastache rugosa* 'Liquorice Blue',
- *Anaphalis margaritacea* 'New Snow',
- *Coreopsis grandiflora* 'Early Sunrise' and 'Sunray',
- *Helenium hoopesii*,
- *Papaver orientale* 'Pizzicato',
- *Rudbeckia fulgida* 'Goldsturm' and *R. triloba*,
- *Verbascum phoeniceum* hybrids.

---

cold areas such half-hardy perennials (HHP) as agapanthus, some fuchsias and many penstemons can benefit from warm, well-drained positions and an insulating winter mulch (see page 92).

As suggested earlier, 'perennial' is a relative term and some hardy perennials are comparatively short-lived, dying out after only a few seasons. Examples include anchusas, forget-me-nots, gaillardias, hollyhocks, sweet rocket (*Hesperis matronalis*), Welsh poppies (*Meconopsis cambrica*), some foxgloves and rudbeckias, perennial honesty (*Lunaria rediviva*) and perennial wallflowers. In unfavourable positions these may behave as biennials.

With their impressive range of colours, forms and sizes, hardy perennials supply the foundation for most beds and borders, but also succeed as container plants, where their absence from the winter scene is acceptable. As permanent members of the garden community they need and deserve due care with soil preparation and choice of site. Many also benefit from periodic overhaul and restoration, especially long-lived kinds that expand into fat congested clumps (see page 82).

BULBS

Bulbs like daffodils, cyclamen and flowering onions (*Allium*) are specialized perennials with distinctive swollen roots or stem bases where they store food to fuel their regrowth after an annual period of rest, which can take place any time of year, depending on their normal flowering season. There is such a diverse range of lifecycles that bulbs can be planted for flowers at every season of the year.

The term 'bulb' includes various kinds of bulbous or allied storage organs such as corms (crocus, colchicum and gladiolus, for example), tubers (dahlias, begonias, arum lilies) and rhizomes, which are simply fleshy creeping stems (bearded irises, lily of the valley,

Many of the seven hundred or so species and countless cultivars of flowering onions (*Allium*) produce immaculate eye-catching spheres of tightly packed blooms that make them the perfect bulb genus for summer highlights on well-drained and sun-drenched soils.

Solomon's seal). Many are permanent garden residents, left in place to flower and gradually spread over a number of years. Others are replanted annually to supply seasonal blooms and then lifted again after their foliage dies down naturally, usually for storage indoors safe from frost or excessively wet conditions. With their straightforward planting and maintenance they are some of the easiest and most versatile flowers for a host of situations, from naturalized patches in lawns or under trees to formal bedding displays in borders and containers.

Most gardeners are familiar with the classic but conservative quartet of early bulbs – crocuses, hyacinths, narcissi and tulips – but bulbs are not just harbingers of spring, and the available repertoire of species and cultivars is huge and constantly growing.

Explore less familiar kinds for some startling discoveries: for example, exotics like sprekelias, eye-

29

catching ginger lilies (*Hedychium*) and the bizarre climbing glory lily (*Gloriosa superba*) for a tropical theme on a warm patio; bluebells, tiny wild ginger (*Asarum*) or, largest of all, the 2.4m (8ft) giant Himalayan lily (*Cardiocrinum giganteum*), all suitable for dappled shade under trees; or alstroemerias, gladioli and florist's anemones (*Anemone coronaria*) to grow in rows for cutting.

Bulbs for special situations

- **Border highlights** *Allium karataviense* and *A. cristophii*, anemones, colchicums, crinums, *Fritillaria imperialis*, galtonias, lilies, nerines, ornithogalums and tulips.
- **Naturalizing in grass** Camassias, crocuses, *Erythronium dens-canis*, *Iris reticulata*, dwarf narcissi, scillas and snake's-head fritillaries (*Fritillaria meleagris*).
- **Under deciduous trees and hedges** *Anemone blanda* and *A. nemorosa*, bluebells, chionodoxa, crocuses, cyclamen, daffodils, erythroniums, scillas, snowdrops, trilliums and winter aconites (*Eranthis*).
- **In damp ground** Camassias, dieramas, erythroniums, fritillaries, *Lilium pardalinum* and *L. superbum*, snowdrops, snowflakes (*Leucojum*), trilliums, *Zantedeschia aethiopica*.

Late-flowering bulbs such as colchicums, autumn crocuses and *Cyclamen hederifolium* (opposite) regularly appear like an encore at the end of the season, a time when most saxifrages, sedums and other rock garden species (right) have finished flowering and are preparing themselves for winter.

SPECIAL GROUPS

Gardeners use a range of other useful categories to identify flowers with specialized qualities or requirements. Although botanically imprecise, these groupings have considerable practical value and convenience when discussing or buying plants for specific sites or purposes.

Alpine and rock plants

In everyday usage these two expressions are interchangeable, and most examples are found muddled together in garden centres and marked simply as 'alpines', but keen gardeners, especially alpine enthusiasts, recognize a distinct difference. A rock garden provides an interesting and congenial home for a wide range of often disparate plants such as prostrate or compact border flowers, miniature bulb hybrids and dwarf or slow-growing shrub cultivars.

Alpines, on the other hand, are very rugged plants from mountainous regions, usually above the tree line where the environment is too harsh for less robust types. As well as being small or prostrate as a survival strategy in bleak, windy surroundings, they have evolved to cope with a spartan existence in freezing temperatures, impoverished soils and a short season of rapid growth. In the relative luxury of an ordinary rock garden they often fall victim to prolonged mildness and damp at times of year when they would normally be hidden under an insulating blanket of snow.

Popular small flowers such as aubrieta, candytuft, thrift

Plants from the water world where early species first evolved supply some of the most arresting and original flowers and foliage: the pink brush heads of persicaria and gunnera's unrestrained leaves (left), for example, or the broad heads of scented stars on *Darmera peltata* (right), which rise high above the pond surface on tall robust stems.

and *Narcissus* 'Tête-à-Tête' all look charming among the rocks and stone mulch of a rock garden, whereas true alpines like androsaces, lewisias, ramondas and soldanellas need frugal, sharply drained growing conditions in a sink, gravel scree bed or 'pavement' of broken flagstones.

Water plants

This group is a huge and diverse community of plants, all sharing a fondness for moist and in some cases waterlogged or totally aquatic surroundings. They vary according to the particular water zone they naturally inhabit and the contribution they make to a balanced pond ecosystem.

- Oxygenating plants are mainly functional but essential species that regulate water chemistry and keep ponds healthy. Most kinds remain submerged and are not noted for their beauty, although one or two such as water violet (*Hottonia palustris*) or water crowfoot (*Ranunculus aquatilis*) have outstanding flowers.

- Floating plants help adjust levels of dissolved nutrients, reducing the risk of algal blooms and 'green water', and shade the surface as they spread and congregate in clusters and rafts. Frogbit (*Hydrocharis morsus-ranae*), vigorous but tender water hyacinth (*Eichornia crassipes*) and the oddly carnivorous bladderwort (*Utricularia vulgaris*) are all worth growing for their blooms.
- Deep-water aquatics, which are generally large plants growing out in the open water, have floating foliage that usefully covers some of the surface and vigorous growth which consumes nutrients and minerals. Water lilies are the best known and most glamorous; other desirable kinds include fragrant water hawthorn (*Aponogeton distachyos*), yellow-flowered Japanese pond lily (*Nuphar japonicum*) and elegant water fringe (*Nymphoides peltata*).
- Marginals and bog plants are multifarious landscaping plants for pond margins or permanently moist ground away from open water. Common perennial flowers like astilbes, hostas, ligularias, mimulus and many primulas grow best here, as well as thirstier *Acorus calamus*, bog arum (*Calla palustris*), *Iris laevigata*, kingcups (*Caltha palustris*) and cardinal flower (*Lobelia cardinalis*).

Bedding plants

'Bedding out' nearly mature plants to provide a seasonal show of flowers and foliage in the garden or in containers is a favourite practice.

Formal bedding

To create a classic summer bedding scheme, start with one or more tall 'dot' plants to give height and a visual centre to the plan. Plant a border of low edging plants all round the perimeter, and then fill the intervening space with groundwork plants of intermediate height.

Dot plants: abutilons, cannas, castor oil plant (*Ricinus*), cordylines, coloured maize and standard fuchsias, heliotrope or pelargoniums.

Edging plants: annual phlox, ageratum, bedding begonias, impatiens, lobelia, pansies, sweet Alison.

Groundwork plants: antirrhinums, asters, calceolarias, dwarf dahlias, French marigolds, mimulus, nemesia, nicotiana, pelargoniums, salvias.

A fitting celebration of summer, with seasonal bedding such as French marigolds and *Begonia semperflorens* densely packed together in a startling, almost riotous carpet of colour, embellished by a simple reflective obelisk.

A variety of flower types are used – half-hardy annuals and perennials for summer displays, hardy biennials and bulbs for spring colour, and sometimes hardy annuals sown direct for spring, summer or autumn flowers – and results can be spectacular and dependable. Some gardeners rely almost exclusively on bedding plants each year, especially brilliant compact upright or trailing varieties for containers and hanging baskets, while others use them to fill gaps in beds and borders with instant short-term colour.

Tender kinds like pelargoniums, petunias, impatiens, lobelia and begonias are among the most popular summer flowers. These need an early start under cover from seeds or cuttings to be ready to start blooming in early summer, although young plants or 'plugs' (see page 71) bought from garden centres and seedsmen are an increasingly popular way to save time, effort and heating costs.

Several kinds of bedding plant are usually combined in a display, which may mean working out some kind of geometric planting scheme to blend and balance different colours, heights and habits in a satisfying combination. Carpet bedding is the intricate art of composing complex pictures and patterns with a whole palette of dwarf bedding plants like echeverias, sedums and sempervivums.

Grasses

With their airy habit, slender foliage and often breathtaking flower displays, ornamental grasses succeed in a variety of roles in the garden, both en masse and as architectural specimens. Plants may be upright, arching or rounded in shape, and bear tiny delicate blooms (most species are wind-pollinated and have no need for extrovert glamour), sometimes packed in great numbers into graceful plumes or branching panicles.

They associate well with large-leaved companions and flat-topped flowers like achilleas, often supplying a long season of interest, even well after their flowers have died and dried on the stems. Their robust growth and vigorous roots make them an ideal choice for colonizing poor soils or for stabilizing steep ground (try dwarf miscanthus, *Panicum virgatum* or *Pennisetum alopecuroides*).

Specimen perennial grasses for containers

Achnatherum (syn. *Stipa*) *calamagrostis* • *Carex siderosticha* 'Variegata' • *Hakonechloa macra* 'Aureola' • *Helictotrichon sempervirens* • *Miscanthus sinensis* cultivars such as 'Flamingo', 'Flammenmeer' or 'Kleine Silberspinne' • *Molinia caerulea* 'Variegata' • *Pennisetum orientale* • *Stipa tenuifolia*.

Some of the varied stars of the *Gramineae*, a family of grasses with many versatile, often undervalued members: panicias and deschampsias, for example, are as graceful and cloudy as a field of oats (left); others, such as the melicas, taller molinias and pennisetums grow in tidy perennial clumps (above).

Both annual and perennial grasses add a natural, almost romantic informality to mixed plantings, and form an essential component of naturalistic schemes (see page 61), whether teamed with native wildflowers or prairie-style perennials such as solidago, monarda, eupatorium, helenium and Japanese anemones.

Some grasses, like andropogon, hakonechloa, molinia and miscanthus, are colourful stars of the autumn

Grasses and wild flowers such as scarlet poppies and white oxeye daisies blend naturally in a small casual drift that needs the simplest maintenance – a single trim to the ground after seed fall will restore order and decorum.

garden, while evergreen carex, deschampsia and sesleria species are essential ingredients of the winter landscape.

Wildflowers

There is no qualitative difference between wildflowers and many cultivated kinds: species and varieties of common garden flowers like dahlias, tulips, clematis and chrysanthemums, for example, grow wild in Mexico, Turkey, North America and China respectively. When gardeners refer to 'wildflowers' they usually mean the indigenous plants of their own country or region, plants that may also be called weeds if they appear uninvited. Some native plants such as primroses, columbines (*Aquilegia*) and lady's mantle (*Alchemilla*) have been grown and appreciated in gardens for centuries.

There are various good reasons for including native wildflowers in any garden plan, apart from their intrinsic charm and beauty. Many species have evolved to survive in very specific locations and therefore make ideal choices for gardens with similar 'difficult' conditions – wet,

acid, chalky or very stony soils, for example. Gardens can be in the frontline of efforts to conserve endangered species: wild places in the countryside are disappearing or threatened in many areas, and with them the plants typically found there. Birds, insects and mammals are at risk, too, as meadows, hedges, thickets and woods disappear, and growing native species is an important contribution to their support, especially in towns where many creatures have sought sanctuary, and will create a wildlife-friendly but still gardenworthy collection of often lovely flowers.

Although not always undemanding or straightforward to grow, most wildflowers enjoy poorer soils, low fertility,

Larger areas can be sown with a balanced mixture of self-sufficient species to produce a richly colourful wildflower meadow with a sequence of flowers. Here lupins, common poppies and ornamental grasses dominate the display.

competition with other plants and similar unfavourable conditions. They can be grown on their own, in containers or small flowering lawns or in exclusive wildflower beds and borders, but are equally happy combined with other (non-native) plants like species roses, mulleins, herbaceous geraniums, and bulbs such as camassias or *Lilium pyrenaicum*.

Flowers for cutting

One of the joys of a lively cosmopolitan flower garden is cutting colourful and varied blooms by the armful for arranging in vases. Gardeners often grow particular kinds for indoor decoration, sometimes allocating rows specially for this purpose to avoid plundering displays elsewhere in the garden. These rows may be sited as edgings to paths or in vegetable beds in back gardens or on allotments. Because they're not part of the garden display tall plants like gladioli, dahlias and chrysanthemums can be supported with canes or wires to keep them straight and upright, while annuals can be sown in batches for cutting in succession. Special

> ## More popular annuals for cutting
>
> Calendula • candytuft • *Chrysanthemum carinatum* and *C. coronarium* varieties • clary • cornflowers • flax (*Linum*)• godetia • gypsophila • larkspur • nigella • scabious • sunflowers • sweet peas • zinnias

varieties have been bred for cutting, such as the extra-tall antirrhinums 'Forerunner' and 'Sky Rocket', aster 'Serenade', cosmos 'Versailles', godetia 'Grace' and sunflower 'Sonja'.

The FLOWER GARDEN

2

Winnowing the best from over a quarter of a million identified flower species, plus countless varieties and cultivars derived from them, might seem a formidable challenge. The first step is to identify those likely to thrive amicably together in a satisfying garden community, supplying maximum pleasure in return for their accommodation and keep. To choose wisely from among these candidates and so compile the most promising shortlist will mean appraising both the garden habitat and your own long-term aspirations.

MAKING YOUR CHOICE

For most gardeners the immediate appeal of a flower will be its appearance, or perhaps some more intangible quality such as its historical associations, scarcity or novelty value – a double Barnhaven primrose, for example, an uncommon laced pink or the world's first multiflora trailing pansy (*Viola* ' Friolina').

Magnetic charm or ancestral associations are not sufficient credentials by themselves, however. Good looks can conceal a fickle temperament and rarity might be explained by a feeble disposition. Constitutional flaws need not disqualify a plant: committed gardeners are sometimes noted for irrationality and a willingness to accept a challenge. But for practical purposes it is always worth approving less obvious qualities such as stamina or hardiness before deciding on a particular plant. Your specific intentions in growing it and the quality of the site (page 55) can also help reduce choice to manageable proportions.

ASSESSING GARDEN MERIT

Find out everything you can about a plant's reputation and performance by consulting a comprehensive encyclopedia of garden flowers to make sure it matches the amount of time and care you can devote to its cultivation. In particular check for the following qualifications:

A thriving flower garden is like a choreographed stage production, using a cast of star performers with various talents, such as the variegated highlights of pelargonium foliage and erigeron's irresponsible carpeting power (foreground, page 40) or the dependable long-season appeal of lady's mantle, white and red valerian (*Centranthus*) and blue campanulas (left)

Vigour Maximum height and spread can be decisive. Allow for these sizes to be exceeded in rich soil, ideal weather or an extended growing season (climate change could become an unpredictable influence on growth). Some flowers are available in a range of tall, intermediate and dwarf varieties to suit different situations (see box on page 44).

Ease of cultivation Find out how much skill and experience might be necessary, both for germination, if growing from seed, and subsequent routine care – one stage of growth can be much easier than the other. Check ease of handling, too: plants may have brittle roots, prickly stems or foliage that sometimes produces allergic reactions.

Sound constitution Weather resistance may be important in some districts or parts of a garden, while immunity to pests or diseases is always helpful, especially for committed organic gardeners seeking alternatives to chemical remedies. Plants with the Award of Garden

A seasoning of tender bedding plants can transform a permanent context of perennials, as here, where scarlet cannas and dahlias add a hint of tropical luxuriance when teamed with bamboos, roses and evergreen striped phormiums.

Exploring varieties

Whereas any variation in a plain species' appearance is probably a reaction to growing conditions, its cultivars will usually have been bred intentionally to differ and meet certain requirements.

For example, the original hollyhock, *Alcea rosea*, is an Asian biennial or short-lived perennial species, 3m (10ft) or more high, with white, pink or mauve single flowers and (once in cultivation) a tendency to suffer from rust. It needs plenty of space, shelter from strong winds, and an infertile soil to prevent ill health.

A modern seed or plant catalogue, however, might offer a number of alternatives. These include shorter varieties from 50cm/20in ('Queeny') upwards, annual forms, double-flowered kinds, mixtures (and single colours) in a range of unusual shades including very nearly black ('Nigra'), as well as close relatives with clear yellow flowers (*A. taurica*) or virtually rust-resistant fig-like leaves (*A. ficifolia*).

Merit (AGM) from the Royal Horticultural Society have been trialled and selected for good constitution and excellent performance without specialist care.

Presentation Consider the plant's appearance when out of bloom, in winter or during a poor spell of weather, for example. Would it need tidying when windswept or frequent deadheading while in flower? As with any proposed relationship, contemplate life with a desirable plant for better or for worse.

DECIDING CRITERIA

In addition to its intrinsic gardenworthiness a potential plant may have to satisfy a more detailed specification, depending on your plans and preferences.

Flower colour is often a top priority, whether to suit your personal likes and dislikes or to fulfil a practical design role – white flowers as highlights in a bed of foliage plants, for example, or hot reds and oranges to add fire to a tropical theme (see page 65). Perennials often differ

by being subtle shades of a particular colour, such as the various blues of many campanulas and herbaceous geraniums; annuals may be available in a whole spectrum of contrasting colours, a blend of more complementary shades or as single colours. Be careful when choosing mixtures of colours: they can sparkle and raise spirits in some contexts but look busy or uninspiring in others.

In addition to colour – possibly their most evident – flowering plants differ dramatically in habit, in distinctive shape and in behaviour. Depending on both species and cultivar (see box page 44), a plant may be tall or dwarf, densely bushy or diffuse, upright, arching, mounded, prostrate or trailing. Structure and profile can be key qualities where the plant is intended to stand alone as a significant feature out of flower as well as in bloom, or to team effectively with its neighbours, perhaps adding bulk and majesty to a border of airy perennials or vertical accents in an otherwise uniform bedding scheme.

Foliage is sometimes overlooked when choosing plants, even though this may be their most enduring feature, playing an active role in the garden before and after flowering. Some plants are grown specifically for their attractive leaves, with their flowers rated as a secondary feature or bonus, but good-looking foliage will enhance the contribution of any flowering plant and may be a deciding factor in a small garden where everything must work hard to merit inclusion. As well as an infinite range of green shades, leaves may be grey or 'silver', red (including purple and bronze shades), yellow or yellow-green, or variegated with contrasting colours. Some plants, like bugle, geraniums or peonies, assume colourful autumn tints, while many plain green plants have interesting leaf shapes and textures – astilbes, incarvillea, nigella and macleaya, for example.

The most glorious flower may seem incomplete or disappointing without a scent, and for many gardeners fragrance is desirable, even essential. Some of the most popular flowers are renowned for their striking and instantly recognizable perfumes, most notably hyacinths, lilies, lily-of-the-valley, pinks, sweet peas and wallflowers. The appeal can be intensely personal – some adore the sweet heady perfume of heliotrope ('cherry pie'), while others find it nauseating. It can also vary between members of the same genus (the rich fragrance of *Lilium regale* compared with the penetrating foxy scent of the yellow Turk's-cap lily, *L. pyrenaicum*) or between cultivars: modern or highly bred forms sometimes sacrifice scent for a more glamorous appearance (antirrhinums, nasturtiums, petunias, scabious) or, like mignonette, have simply lost it over the years. Perfume is usually intensified in warm still air and confined surroundings such as an enclosed patio.

MATCHING PLANTS TO PURPOSE

Recognizing the behaviour and even the idiosyncrasies of different flowers can help you place them to best effect in the garden. Sometimes a particular type is the perfect answer for planting up a difficult site (see page 57), or its specialized habit the ideal match for an exacting purpose, which might vary from disguising an eyesore to adding colour and interest to bare ground at the foot of a hedge.

Plants for walls

Many popular and effective climbers such as ivy, wisteria or Virginia creeper are woody perennials and beyond the scope of this book. They may also take several seasons to cover a large area, which is where annual and herbaceous perennial climbers excel. Annuals like tall sweet peas, thunbergia, climbing nasturtiums and morning glories (*Ipomoea*) can fill wall space rapidly while woody kinds are still maturing; add to these such perennials as *Aconitum hemsleyanum* and *A. volubile*, clematis of all kinds, codonopsis, hops (*Humulus*) and the irrepressible everlasting sweet peas *Lathyrus grandiflorus* and *L. latifolius*. Consider plants that naturally grow in rocky sites for filling gaps on walls: sow or plant erigeron, lewisias, ivy-leaved toadflax (*Cymbalaria muralis*) and ordinary wallflowers direct in cracks and crevices.

Although sometimes undervalued by sophisticated gardeners, pelargoniums remain some of the most popular bedding flowers, not least for massing in dry sun-drenched spots, where the relatively trouble-free plants supply colour all summer or longer in return for little attention.

Some flowers naturally aim high: morning glory (left), a vigorous twiner whose beautiful blooms unfurl from long buds at the touch of the morning sun; scarlet flame creeper sneaking brightly through a mid-season clematis (centre); and the white form of red valerian, *Centranthus ruber* (right), a zealous colonizer of walls high or low.

Simple ingredients often make the most successful and pleasing late-spring ground-cover combination, as here, where a handful of slender lily-flowered tulips embellishes a rich green weed-suppressant mat of white daisies.

Covering ground

Plants that comprehensively blanket the ground can smother most weeds, conserve moisture and even bind loose soil together (on steep banks, for example), as well as spread a gently undulating carpet or more diffuse meadow layer of foliage and flowers beneath taller perennials and shrubs. Vigorous kinds like *Lamium galeobdolon*, which rapidly colonizes whole swathes of ground, are valuable for large gardens but may be too rampant in smaller spaces. More restrained flowering examples include *Achillea tomentosa*, *Aurinia saxatilis*, *Anthemis nobilis*, *Iberis sempervirens*, *Phlox subulata*, *Saponaria ocymoides*, tiny raoulia for paved areas, heucheras, arabis, stachys and various geraniums.

Easy-care plants

Creating a successful low-maintenance garden requires a unified plan that combines a number of techniques such as mulching, close spacing, balancing plant communities to reduce health problems and an emphasis on minimum-care surfaces. When identifying self-reliant

Flowering roofs

Planting on the roof of a shed, garage or porch can extend the garden area into otherwise wasted space and improve the locale, especially in towns, by reducing the run-off of storm water, absorbing carbon dioxide and air pollutants, cooling the immediate surroundings and masking a possibly ugly building surface. It will also protect and insulate the roof itself. The structure may need reinforcement, although total weight of soil, plants and barrier membranes against roots and water need not exceed that of a gravel roof, typically about 80kg per sq. m (210lb per sq. yd). Depending on the depth of soil (consult a specialist handbook for mixtures and quantities) you could grow shallow-rooted rock plants like sedum, sempervivums and thyme or larger grassland species such as bird's-foot trefoil, common mallow, fumitory and maiden pinks.

plants, concentrate on those that seem likely to enjoy your soil and climate (see pages 55–6), need the least staking, clipping, pruning and general tidying, and supply maximum colour and appeal throughout the year. Restrained trees and shrubs, many of them evergreen, might comprise the skeleton of your plan, but you could also include undemanding perennials like bergenias, hellebores, hostas, irises such as dwarf-bearded *Iris pumila* and the Siberian iris *I. sibirica*, Welsh poppies (*Meconopsis cambrica*) to self-seed in otherwise inhospitable spots, peonies (which thrive on being left alone) and a range of primulas. Add hardy and half-hardy annuals for instant and disposable highlights.

Sensitive use of colour can complement or modify a garden's impact: warm or subdued reds that partner roses without competing for attention (left), for example, the soft blue foliage and pastel flowers of hostas that blend into lightly shaded surroundings (above), or lively reds, brash golds and gleaming yellows that add fiery highlights to a hot border (right).

Themed gardens

Another popular aim is the creation of a special style. One example is a tropical paradise where you could choose large-leaved perennials like ricinus, nicandra or rodgersia with red, orange and yellow summer bedding. Another might be a semi-formal Japanese design using a context of natural accessories such as rock, wood and water in which to set a few outstanding and authentic

A satisfying community of flowers that co-exist amicably in a hot, dry site: alliums, phlomis and veronicas, planted in naturalistic, informal drifts through a mulch of gravel, make a resilient partnership.

plants (explore species whose names end with *asiatica*, *chinensis*, *japonica*, *orientalis* or *sinensis*).

THE RIGHT PLACES FOR PLANTS

The final and definitive test of the ideal plant is its constitutional fitness for the site. Whether it will be happy in its intended home can depend on a number of factors that may not be instantly apparent to you or even seem particularly important. For the plant, however, they may be crucial.

Climate

Although some plants seem content to grow almost anywhere (many of these are called weeds), most have a strong preference for a site that is predominantly warm or cool, wet or dry, sometimes at specific times of year.

One of the most important qualities to check is a plant's hardiness. To most gardeners a hardy plant is one that withstands frost, but the term is relative and can mean

Flowers for drying

Flower arrangers use an enormous selection of plants to supply fresh cut flowers. Towards the end of the season the choice may extend to appealing seed heads and a specialized range of long-lasting flowers, which preserve their colour, shape and papery texture almost indefinitely when dried. Most are easily grown annual sun-lovers, including varieties of anaphalis, catananche, clary (*Salvia viridis*), gomphrena, helipterum, statice (*Limonium*), straw flower (*Bracteantha bracteata*) and xeranthemum. These are often sold as a mixture of 'everlasting flowers' or 'immortelles'.

various things in different countries or districts. In Australia, for example, 'hardy' means drought and salt tolerant.

In the USA huge regional differences in climate led to the formulation of hardiness zones, defined by the typical average lowest winter temperature. A zone 8 plant for example, hardy down to −12C (10°F), is unlikely to survive in Minnesota, a zone 4 region where temperatures can fall to −34C (−30°F). The UK is mainly Z8 with areas of warmer Z9 near coasts (and in London), but a cold Z7 winter is not unknown. Many reference books and catalogues use this system as a rough guide to selecting suitable plants.

Acidity and alkalinity

Use a simple test kit from a garden centre to check the amount of calcium in your soil and help define its type: acid soil contains less calcium, alkaline soils more.

Some plants are not particularly fussy, others like a neutral soil about midway between the two extremes, but many have a firm preference for one type over the other.

- Lime-loving (calcicole) flowers for alkaline or chalky soil: aster, campanula, dianthus, fuchsia, narcissus, poppies, tulips, verbascum, vinca and individual species like *Lilium candidum* and *L. martagon,* or *Geranium macrorrhizum.*
- Ericaceous (calcifuge or acid-loving) flowers: asclepias, begonias, blue poppies (*Meconopsis*), calceolarias, dierama, erythronium, fritillary, lupins, primulas, sanguinaria, trillium, and *Lilium speciosum* and *L. tigrinum.*

Every garden has its own microclimate, which may be warmer or cooler than those near by; even different parts of the same plot can vary considerably, while town gardens are generally warmer than those in country districts and can be totally frost-free. Be prepared to experiment with doubtful or borderline plants, and possibly move them later to a more congenial position: a sunny or shaded aspect on a different side of the house or garden might make all the difference. The unpredictability of climate change could turn growing some present certainties into a gamble in the future.

Soil

Unless you grow plants in containers (see page 66), where you can easily tailor an appropriate rooting mix, the nature of your ground will favour or eliminate whole groups of flowers. Depending on their origins, different kinds have a strong preference for soil characteristics like slow or fast drainage, low or high fertility and levels of acidity (see box, left). It is possible to amend soil to a limited extent – by adding grit for improved drainage, perhaps, or organic matter for extra humus and nutrients – but very often it is easier and, in the long term, more successful to choose plants adapted to your existing conditions.

Draining heavy ground, for example, can be an expensive and disruptive undertaking compared with accepting the situation as an opportunity to grow damp-loving perennials like astilbe, filipendula, gentian, ligularia, monarda, polygonum and trollius. Hot dry ground, especially in full sun, would please achillea, centranthus, crocosmia, gaillardia, pyrethrum, salvia, evening primroses (*Oenothera*) and a host of bedding annuals without much alteration.

Difficult sites

Many gardeners judge their ground or surroundings to be 'difficult', which can sometimes mean little more than unsuitable for a chosen range of plants. It is a rare garden that will host every kind of plant without some amendment – shelter for fragile and refined species on windswept sites, a raised bed for drought-sensitive kinds in shallow soil over chalky subsoil or remedial pruning to relieve heavy tree shadow above summer bedding, for example. But a combination of environmental improvement and careful selection of compatible plants should produce a working solution without seriously limiting choice.

There are extensive ranges of plants that revel in tough conditions like heavy clay, dry shade, gravel drives, polluted atmospheres, light hungry soils, acid bogs or the

The success of a seaside garden depends on the selection of robust flowers that happily tolerate salt-laden winds as well as often intense sunshine and sea mists, sheltered behind a 'sea defence' of resilient windbreak shrubs, such as sea buckthorn or evergreens like escallonia and griselinia.

Seaside gardens

Flowers in gardens by the sea need to be rugged, able to shrug off salt spray and buffeting or desiccation from frequent high winds in an otherwise genial climate of sunshine and warmth. Successful plants defend themselves with a variety of adaptations: hairy, leathery or succulent foliage with small, slender or grey leaves, and stems that are flexible or very short. Provide shelter with resilient shrubs and hedges, and then plant flowers like amaryllis, catananche, *Crambe cordifolia*, crocosmia, dierama, euphorbia, kniphofia, limonium, thrift, osteospermum, phormium, polygonum, salvia, *Senecio pulcher* and wallflowers.

Successful plant combination techniques may use an airy flower such as *Verbena bonariensis* (left) to contribute diffuse colour without obscuring or diminishing its neighbours, or partner the main star with strong colour contrasts and harmonies, as here (right), where golden phlomis and rich yellow roses make a perfect team.

crevices of a dilapidated pavement. Many more can tolerate such positions, if not altogether rejoice in them.

Even a waste ground of builders' rubble, stones and exhausted soil is an inviting habitat for buoyant pioneer plants, which will quickly establish a dynamic and colourful community. Easy-going favourites like amaranthus, borage, crocus, columbines, foxgloves, pot marigolds, hellebores, honesty, forget-me-nots, violets, red valerian and orange-flowered hawkweeds (*Hieracium*) can all romp along on a meagre diet and will self-seed to fill the space with new spontaneous colonies.

DESIGNING WITH FLOWERS

A generation or two ago most flowers were planted according to prescribed styles. Perennials tended to be grown in herbaceous borders, sometimes on a lavish scale, where plants were carefully graded according to height, colour or flowering season.

Annual bedding plants were arranged in formal geometrical patterns (see page 33) of contrasting heights and harmonious colours. Even the 'cottage garden' style, sometimes perceived as an artless medley of flowers gathered together in cheerful anarchy, was in reality often a carefully stage-managed composition following a few standard formulae.

Happily a kind of post-modern rejection of rules has refreshed garden planning, breaking old moulds with a sense of freedom and willingness to experiment. Some

Celebrate the richness and diversity of the flower palette with some of the garden's less obvious choices: the busy angularity and subtle shades of allium seed heads and sea holly (left); sumptuous bold bergenia foliage making bold contrasts with daintier spring bulbs (near right); the soft cream spires of double camassias (centre right); or the brooding warmth of some sedum cultivars (far right).

basic guidelines on combining plants (see page 64) are still valuable, but personal inspiration is as acceptable as conforming with custom. The plants themselves are more widely respected these days as individuals with personalities of their own rather than just passive ingredients in a planting recipe.

Study traditional genres and classic gardens open to the public for helpful ideas to blend with your own criteria, which may be a partiality for certain flower types and colours, a specific purpose such as encouraging wildlife or adding shapely set pieces to a contemporary setting, or simply a desire to achieve a profusion of flowers with the least maintenance. Orthodox planting styles were often labour-intensive, not least because plants tend to wander or self-seed out of line and find more inviting habitats. This natural evolution can be more successful than imposing a conformist plan.

NATURAL GARDENING

The contrived appearance of many traditional styles and the amount of work involved in looking after them can be replaced with a more informal approach that echoes the kind of plant communities found in the wild. A broad mix of flowers matching the environmental conditions in your garden can be more stable and productive than a rigid scheme on an unsuitable site, and could require little upkeep beyond an annual tidy.

Beds and borders

Grow spreading flowers like coreopsis, *Lychnis coronaria*, hardy salvias, monarda and sidalcea in generous, relaxed drifts and let them merge and interlace to suppress weeds and provide mutual support. Plan varieties for seasonal harmonies, adding earlier- and later-flowering kinds wherever necessary for a long progression of attractive flowers and foliage.

A prairie garden

Typical prairie flowers are sturdy, self-reliant species that can make a dramatic impact in large borders or smaller suburban gardens, wherever there is space and fertile soil. Choose strongly coloured plants like eupatorium, echinacea, heliopsis and vernonia for large spaces, or smaller asters, geums, filipendula and liatris in more confined areas. Interplant their bold groups with stout

Bold drifts of compatible perennials that meet, mingle and provide each other with mutual support (left) are a low-maintenance solution to filling large areas with flowers and foliage. The same principle can be applied to lawns (opposite), reserving areas planted with bulbs and wildflowers for only occasional mowing once blooming and seeding are over.

grasses (arundo, carex, miscanthus, for example), and cut everything down at the end of the season, in late autumn for tidiness or late winter after their display of seed heads.

Lawns and meadows

Where the soil is less fertile, consider establishing a naturalized mixture of easy-going flowers like anthemis, asters, linum, origanum, pulsatilla, scabious and sedums with a selection of attractive grasses to make a perennial meadow. In smaller gardens or where tidiness is important, choose the shortest species, add drifts and patches of bulbs like crocus and narcissi, and mow at 4–5cm (1½–2in) high from mid-summer onwards once ripe seeds have been shed. Cut wilder meadows at mid-

A flower for every day

By choosing plants according to their flowering season, it is possible to build a collection that will offer some colour all year round. Here is just a small selection of less familiar but dependable kinds.

Spring Brunnera, comfrey (*Symphytum*), foam flower (*Tiarella*), knapweed (*Centaurea*), navelwort (*Omphalodes*), pheasant's eye (*Adonis*), Siberian wallflower (*Erysimum* x *allionii*), Solomon's seal (*Polygonatum* x *hybridum*), speedwell (*Veronica*).

Summer Achillea, alstroemeria, anchusa, *Crambe cordifolia*, foxtail lily (*Eremurus*), goat's beard (*Aruncus*), hemerocallis, inula, masterwort (*Astrantia*), meadow rue (*Thalictrum*), mulleins (*Verbascum*), penstemon, sea holly (*Eryngium*).

Autumn Cardinal flower (*Lobelia cardinalis*), culver's root (*Veronicastrum virginicum*), globe thistle (*Echinops*), Japanese anemones, liriope, loosestrife (*Lythrum*), monkshood (*Aconitum*), mugwort (*Artemisia*), snakeroot (*Cimicifuga*), tree poppy (*Romneya*), vervain (*Verbena*).

Winter See page 101.

summer, remove all the cuttings and then allow plants to grow unchecked again for the rest of the season.

COMBINING FLOWERS

The overall impression of a garden scheme can depend on sensitively partnering plants so that they work together rather than in competition with each other, balancing their appearance and flowering season with the form and texture of their foliage to make a satisfying tableau. Choreographing plants of different shapes can achieve quite dramatic effects: use tall slender spires of flowers to frame a rounded perennial or emphasize a view, for example, or stud a uniform froth of small branching flower stems with spikes of lupins or the neat spheres of allium heads.

The form of a plant is often a guide to the best way to use it. Low ground-cover and prostrate plants like epimediums or vincas need massing in generous groups for impact, whereas a single erect grass or bulky plant like a peony can make a significant contribution on its own among more compact or self-effacing neighbours. Flowering season can suggest partnerships: plants like primulas and pulmonarias bloom while late summer neighbours such as phlox or rudbeckias are still small or invisible, and then they welcome the shade cast by the latecomers as these take their turn.

Plant densities may be influenced by your budget and

Examples of different habits

Spiky flowers Delphiniums, eremurus, galega, hollyhocks, *Iris ochroleuca*, kniphofia, liriope, lupins, monkshood, physostegia, *Sisyrinchium striatum*.

Bulky clumps Achillea, cardoons (*Cynara cardunculus*), hosta, lavatera, monarda, phlox, Rubellum chrysanthemums, symphytum.

Light airy flowers Agastache, aquilegia, *Gypsophila paniculata*, heuchera, limonium, London pride (*Saxifraga* x *urbium*), thalictrum, *Verbena bonariensis* and *V. hastata*.

Bold daisies asters, anthemis, erigeron, helenium, heliopsis, Korean chrysanthemums, pyrethrum (*Tanacetum coccineum*), Shasta daisies (*Leucanthemum* x *superbum*).

Good blues are rare shades that many gardeners prefer to mass on their own for maximum impact. Just a few *Allium cristophii* seedheads, for example, supply intriguing starry highlights without diluting this rich display of blue perennial flax.

patience. Initial close planting is more expensive but can result in a presentable display in the first year, especially with rapidly established perennials like anchusa, monarda or Michaelmas daisies. Surplus plants can be sacrificed or transplanted later when congestion threatens. Alternatively plant at final spacings – small perennials about 20–23cm (8–9in) apart, larger kinds 30–40cm (12–16in) and vigorous individuals like peonies 60–90cm (2–3ft) apart – and then fill the intervening gaps with annuals for the first season. Aim for an average density of 4–5 plants per square metre, or 7–10 for smaller kinds like heucheras and violets. Custom used to advise planting varieties in groups of odd numbers, typically three, five or seven (for this reason perennials are often sold in these multiples at a discount), but this is not mandatory, especially in limited spaces, and is only useful for achieving a faster natural appearance.

Composing with colour

Flower and foliage colours can be used to lift a display or make an extravagant gesture. Harmonious colour

schemes can be cool or restful, but without the odd contrast of primary colours may seem bland in poor light. Play with a colour chart to explore effects, noting how for instance orange can add piquancy to light green or a touch of white can stress the depth of a rich red scheme.

Some single colours have a particular fascination and can look impressive when used as a theme for a whole monochrome bed or border.

- White flowers are a classic choice for a special collection, producing an impression of melancholy dreaminess or brightening a dark shady corner of the garden until well after dark. Their successful combination needs a keen eye for size, shape and texture as well as their subtle variation in shade and intensity.
- Blue suggests depth, distance and cool relief from heat, and is a colour for which bees seem to have a decided preference. A popular colour, it remains visible to the human eye long after sunset. In its purest form, free from pink or mauve tints, it is rare and highly prized.
- Green flowers have a special appeal for florists and flower arrangers, but for others they are an acquired taste, partly because so many shades of green already fill the backdrop of foliage in most gardens. Subtle and soothing in their impact, green flowers tend to be wind pollinated and so have no need to advertise their

presence with glitter or gloss, but some (such as mignonette and green forms of nicotiana) have a seductive perfume.

- Black as applied to flowers is something of a misnomer, since true black is not found in the plant world, and most examples are in fact deep purple, inky blue or dusky reddish-brown hybrids. Some find them sinister or funereal, but used with discrimination they have a plush and intriguing effect.

Remember no colour is seen in isolation in a garden, however: any colour will usually have a green background.

FLOWERS IN CONTAINERS

Pots and other containers were historically reserved for tender plants unable to survive outdoors all year, but their use today is universal, for all kinds of plants from alpines and summer bedding to massive clumps of perennial grasses, bamboos and even trees. They can inject supplementary colour and seasonal highlights into flower beds and borders, supply conditions quite different from those of the open ground or allow plants to be grown where no other garden exists – on a patio, roof top or balcony, for example.

Almost any kind of flower can be grown successfully in a container provided it has enough compost of the appropriate kind, has adequate drainage at the base and

Containers of appropriate sizes can offer congenial homes for most flower types, including long-term foliage plants like these striped agaves and tender succulents, and more seasonal stalwarts such as pelargoniums and lilies.

receives due care with watering and feeding. Plants in pots are almost totally dependent on regular attention for their welfare, which can involve daily watering in hot dry weather and feeding every seven to ten days once compost nutrients are exhausted (about six weeks after potting).

Annual or biennial repotting to replace old compost with a fresh supply is an opportunity to divide perennials and keep them young and vigorous, while tender kinds can be moved between indoors and the open air according to the time of year and prevailing weather. Hardy and half-hardy annuals can be sown or planted in pots indoors for moving outside to flower as the weather improves – an advantage in colder districts where the growing season is short.

Specialist plant groups can be collected in sympathetic containers where garden conditions are unsuitable or to display them to greater advantage. Examples are: difficult alpines in a stone sink of gritty free-draining compost; aquatic plants in a miniature water garden created in a half barrel; or a tub of assorted spring bulbs to flower in sequence center stage, before being transplanted to garden beds or retired out of sight when blooms finally fade.

3

STARTING
with
FLOWERS

Armed with an understanding of your environmental
conditions and a wish list of ideal plants, you are
ready to start assembling the star cast of your
proposed show. Whether you choose to buy them
as growing plants or raise them from seed, or
combine both methods, there are simple and
trustworthy ways to achieve success and ensure
the creation of a rewarding flower garden that will
evolve and give you pleasure for years to come.

BUYING PLANTS

All the different types of flowering plants can be bought at various stages of growth, from recently germinated seedlings to mature specimens in full bloom. The readily available range may be limited to the most popular kinds. Less common and recently introduced varieties often cost more or need searching out, and you may need to investigate several sources to gather together all the plants on your shopping list.

Plant sources

Garden centres These usually retail a wide selection of staple varieties, especially bedding plants and hardy perennials; larger centres will stock more unusual kinds. You may find inexpensive seedlings and young plants, but the majority will be in flower to stimulate impulse buying. Don't necessarily expect authoritative advice.

Specialist nurseries The best sources of rarer plants as well as more familiar varieties, all usually grown on site by experienced specialists who can help you make your choice. Many offer a catalogue and mail-order service, although you then need to allow for carriage costs and anticipate dealing with plants on delivery, especially if they are bare-rooted.

What to look for

Healthy, vigorous and well-tended stock can save you a lot of worry and effort later, so inspect choices carefully before buying. Reject any with:

- sickly, wilting, discoloured or 'drawn' (elongated) leaves or stems, which can be symptoms of ill health, starvation or overcrowding;
- pots with compost that is dry, densely weedy or green with surface algae, suggesting under- or over-watering and general poor maintenance;
- split or unlabelled containers and any with thick or numerous roots protruding at the base: plants may be injured, potbound or impostors.

A mixed border is the ideal solution for a modern garden, its blend of trees, shrubs and flowering or fruiting hedges framing hardy perennials and seasonal bedding like this collection of dahlias (page 68), offering background colour and structure all year round.

Markets and stalls Quality may vary widely, with limited selection and unreliable naming, but plants are usually inexpensive, even cut price. Stalls at national, local and specialist club shows are an excellent source of rarities, novelties and heritage plants from past generations.

Friends Like all enthusiasts, gardeners can be extraordinarily generous, willingly donating or exchanging spare plants and cuttings: many old varieties have survived and multiplied in this informal way. Check gifts for unwelcome extras like perennial weed fragments, and beware the 'wonderful' ground-cover plant that becomes a well-dressed thug in your soil or the 'unusual' flower which might be infected with transmissible virus disease.

Stages of growth

Plants can be offered for sale at various stages of growth. Which stage you choose is usually reflected in the price (the older the plant, the more you will pay) and the amount of aftercare it will need.

Seedlings The youngest, least expensive and also the most demanding because they will require pricking out (see page 80) to give them more space and sustenance. For steady healthy growth you must be able to provide good light and possibly heat, depending on the type of plant and time of year. This is the best way to buy a variety in large quantities, usually multiples of a hundred.

Plug plants These are seedlings or rooted cuttings that are separate and well rooted in multi-cellular trays or packed separately if mailed. They range in size (mini-, standard and large plugs) according to age or plant habit. The smallest can be transferred to 8cm (3in) pots or planted direct into hanging baskets; the biggest are usually ready for larger containers or the open garden after hardening off (see pages 86–7).

Young plants A little older still, these can take a variety of forms, from flowering bedding in Jiffy pots (mesh-clad peat blocks) and plants in plastic or polystyrene trays and strips, to bushy juveniles in 8–10cm (3–4in) pots. All may be planted straight out or potted on for a few weeks until conditions outside are favourable.

Mature plants These may be container grown and ready for planting whenever convenient, or bare-root stock that on arrival will usually need soaking for a few hours in water before being potted or planted before the roots dry out again.

GROWING FROM SEED

This is the cheapest and, for many gardeners, the most satisfying way to raise large numbers of a particular plant, and sometimes the only option for rare or unusual kinds. Results are predictable with all species and natural

Easy multiplication

- Before settling acquisitions into their final homes, look to see if you can produce a few more plants with little effort or extra outlay.
- Non-flowering shoots on bushy bedding plants could yield cuttings to root quickly and bring into flower the same season (see pages 82–3).
- Pot up trailing perennials and bedding plants, and peg down the ends of their long stems to root and then detach as layers (see page 86).
- Multi-stemmed clumps can sometimes be split and potted up or planted out separately (see page 82). Overgrown perennials sold at a discount after flowering will often divide into several portions.

Some of the brightest flowers are the easiest to raise from seed – annual opium poppies and biennial foxgloves (left), for example; even perennial astilbes (above) may be sown, although named cultivars should be divided and must be introduced as growing plants.

varieties but are not reliable – except in a very few instances – for cultivars, most of which are propagated vegetatively instead (see pages 80–86), using portions of plant tissue such as cuttings or divisions to ensure the offspring are identical. Sowing routines vary according to the type of plant and time of year.

Hardy annuals

Most kinds are sown outdoors in early spring for summer flowering, or in autumn for earlier flowers the following year. Earlier sowing under glass will advance flowering, especially in colder areas, while short-lived annuals like linaria, nigella and night-scented and Virginia stocks (*Matthiola*) can be sown two to three times from spring to mid-summer for continuity.

Hardy biennials and perennials

These are sown outdoors in late spring or early summer in a prepared seed bed and then thinned out or transplanted to an extra piece of ground to allow each plant more space to develop. They are planted out in their flowering positions in early and mid-autumn, or early the following spring in cold or wet areas. Hardy perennials may also be sown under glass in the same way as half-hardy kinds for blooms the same year.

Half-hardy annuals and perennials

As it is not safe to sow these outside until after the last frosts, they are started in gentle warmth indoors in late winter or early spring so that plants on the point of flowering will be ready to go out as the risk of frost recedes.

INDOOR SOWING METHODS

Apart from the seeds themselves, you will need two essential items of equipment: an appropriate compost and a suitable container. Choose a compost grade intended for propagation (a soil-less 'seeds and cuttings' mix or soil-

Some flower seeds require very precise treatment. These South African leucospermums, for example, belong to a group of protea relatives that naturally germinate only after wild fires, and their seeds will not grow unless exposed to smoke: either use special smoke preparations for watering the seeds or buy growing plants in early summer.

Sowing schedule

- **Late winter** Half-hardy perennials such as begonias, pelargoniums and petunias indoors in heat.
- **Early to mid-spring** Half-hardy annuals such as tagetes, nicotiana, gazanias indoors in heat; hardy annuals like lavatera, echium, larkspur outdoors.
- **Late spring/early summer** Hardy biennials (campanulas, Brompton stocks, Iceland poppies) and all hardy perennials outdoors.
- **Early autumn** Hardy annuals like sweet peas, candytuft (*Iberis*) and calendula outdoors or in a cold frame.

based John Innes seed compost), and avoid unnecessary problems by making sure it is fresh, moist and warmed to room temperature. Containers should be clean plastic trays, wooden boxes, or clay or plastic pots: choose a size that matches the quantity and size of the seeds.

You may also need water at room temperature and a bowl or a watering can fitted with a very fine rose; a fine sieve or riddle; clean seed labels and a pencil; glass, plastic film or a propagator to maintain moist conditions; and vermiculite to cover seeds.

Sowing steps

1. Fill the container with compost and level the top by striking off the excess with a ruler or seed label. Tap the container on the working surface to settle soil-less compost; lightly firm a soil-based mix with a piece of wood (for trays) or a jam jar for pots.

2. Gently water the prepared container by can from above, or stand it in a bowl of shallow water until damp patches appear on the surface. Put aside for an hour or so while surplus water drains.

3. Pour seeds into one hand and use the finger and thumb of the other to scatter them very thinly and evenly over the surface. Larger seeds can be spaced at regular intervals apart.

4. Sift a thin sprinkling of compost over the seeds, except any that need light for germination (begonias, cuphea, petunias), which should be pressed gently into the surface or covered with a thin layer of vermiculite.

5. Label the container with variety, date and supplier, and then place it in a propagator preset to the required temperature, or cover it with glass or plastic film and keep in a warm place: 15C (60°F) is a sound average temperature unless the packet advises otherwise.

6. Check every day or so that the compost is still moist, and wipe any condensation from covers. If you need to water before seedlings appear, stand containers in about 2.5cm (1in) of water at room temperature until this is seen to soak through to the surface.

7. Watch out for first signs of emergence: the majority of common flowers take one to three weeks to appear, but some need much longer, especially in cool surroundings.

8. Once seedlings begin to emerge, uncover and move containers into good light (but not bright sunshine) and keep at a lower temperature, around 10C (50°F) to prevent soft sappy growth.

Alternative methods

Once seedlings are large enough to handle they need pricking out individually (see page 80). You can avoid this stage with some flowers by modifying the basic sowing technique.

- Tiny seedlings like lobelia are usually pricked out in small clusters for faster, bulkier plants, and this is much easier if seeds are sown in rows across a tray to emerge as a slim 'hedge' of seedlings.
- Large seeds like sweet peas, castor oil plant and acanthus can be sown individually in small pots (especially paper or Jiffy types that decay in the soil) for growing on to planting size without further disturbance.
- Similarly, smaller seeds can be sown in small pots or the cells of a divided tray, a tiny pinch in each, and left unthinned to make bushy clumps at planting time.

OUTDOOR SOWING METHODS

Seeds of hardy flowers may be sown where they are to grow or in a temporary nursery bed for transplanting later. In both cases a clean, weed-free seed bed with a fine tilth (a well-broken surface) is essential. Wait until the soil is warm enough to break up easily – the emergence of new weed seedlings is a reliable cue – and then use a rake to tamp and level the surface to an open and even crumbly texture.

Keep the rake handy for sowing the seeds; you may also need a garden line, a watering can, labels and a pencil.

Direct sowing outdoors suits many flowers, especially hardy annuals or a sparkling mixture of wild flowers like these, sown in bold patches in an ornamental collection of vegetables.

Sowing tips

- All seeds need adequate warmth, air and moisture, and a shortage or excess of these factors can delay or suppress germination. A few plants also need special treatments such as pre-soaking or a period of freezing.
- Flowers sown when weather conditions improve often catch up those sown earlier and possibly held back by the cold.
- Sow as sparsely as possible: this can prevent overcrowding and even save transplanting or thinning seedlings later.
- Sowing too deeply is a common cause of failure. The rule of thumb is to cover seeds with a depth of compost equal to their diameter.
- Seedlings with long tap roots (poppies, eschscholzias) resent transplanting and must be sown where they are to flower or in pots for planting out undisturbed.
- Use mains water for indoor seeds and seedlings, because rainwater from butts can carry potentially lethal pathogens such as damping off disease.

Sowing steps

1. Use the corner of the rake head (or a hoe, trowel or stick) to draw shallow channels or 'drills' on the surface. Sowing in straight parallel rows makes weeding easier, so use a garden line or the edge of a board to guide the drills. Follow seed packet instructions for distances between rows, or space them 15cm (6in) apart as a practical average. If the soil is dry, flood each drill with water from a can.

2. Tip a quantity of seeds into one hand and take a pinch at a time, sprinkling them thinly into the drill from between the finger and thumb of the other hand. Large seeds can be spaced out at final distances apart, with a few spares at the end of the drill for gapping up direct sowings in borders.

3. Use the rake or your hand to draw a little soil over the seeds from the side of the drill, and gently firm this in place with the rake head held vertically. In hot dry weather and on poor or heavy soils, the seeds can be covered with moist garden compost, leafmould or potting compost. Label each row, check regularly for signs of emergence or disturbance, and water drills with a fine rose in dry weather.

Alternative techniques

The basic method is suitable when sowing in a nursery bed or a large patch to make a bold display. For small quantities or when filling in odd gaps between other

In temperate climates most half-hardy annuals require early sowing indoors or should be bought as young plants. Tender *Cleome hassleriana* (syn. *spinosa*), for example, are started in late winter or early spring to allow enough time for plants to reach flowering stage by the longest day.

plants, use an inverted 13–15cm (5–6in) pot to impress a circular drill in the soil.

Seeds may be broadcast (scattered randomly but evenly) across a large area or over a smaller, more precise target, and either raked lightly into the soil or covered with a shallow sprinkling of fine compost. This works for wildflower seeds when sowing a mini-meadow, and for patches of naturalized garden flowers like limnanthes to attract bees or forget-me-nots around and over peonies for a combination of blue flowers and red foliage. Broadcast annuals like nigella or phacelia over spring bulbs to hide their dying foliage in a thicket of cheerful blooms.

Autumn-sown annuals are usually started in an outdoor nursery bed, but in colder districts they can benefit from being sown in a cold frame for protection over winter. Either broadcast or sow in drills in a soil-based frame; or sow a pinch of seeds per 13cm (5in) pot and leave all the seedlings to grow. Hold back a few potfuls for early display in a cool greenhouse or indoors on a windowsill.

MANAGING SEEDLINGS

Most flower seedlings emerge with a pair of plain 'seed leaves' first and then produce more typical true leaves (grasses and grass-like plants have only one seed leaf, though). When the true leaves start to appear, seedlings require more space to develop individually; otherwise they compete against each other, with inevitable casualties. The next stage of growing from seed involves giving the seedlings the elbow room they need for healthy unrestricted growth.

Pricking out

Unless sown with plenty of room – in cell trays or small pots, for example – seedlings raised under glass are transplanted (pricked out) into pots or trays for growing on to planting stage. Large vigorous kinds such as dahlias, cosmos, nasturtiums or African marigolds can be moved individually into 8–9cm (3–3½in) pots; smaller seedlings are spaced about 5cm (2in) apart in seed trays. Wait until you can manipulate the seedlings easily, and always handle them by holding a leaf rather than the stem, which is easily crushed.

Fill pots and trays as for sowing, using a universal soil-less mix or John Innes No. 1 potting compost. Carefully loosen and separate seedlings with a dibber, pencil or old table fork, and transfer each to a dibber hole in the compost, large enough to take the roots comfortably. Gently firm seedlings in place at the depth they were growing before, and water completed containers with a fine rose. Stand them in good light but not direct sun, and keep consistently moist.

Thinning

You can achieve the same result by removing or pinching off surplus seedlings to leave the remainder at 5cm (2in)

There is rarely any difficulty raising crocosmia species, which steadily spread into fat clumps that need periodic division or chopping back with a sharp spade. Cultivars such as rich red 'Lucifer' (right) are slightly more restrained than the vigorous common orange montbretia.

spacings where they have been sown, causing little or no check to the growth of those left in place. This can be done with all seedlings, whether in trays or the open ground.

Once plants in trays have bushed out and nearly touch each other they can usually be planted out after any necessary hardening off (see pages 86–7). The same applies to those in a nursery bed, or you could transplant them 15cm (6in) apart to make larger specimens for final planting in autumn (mild areas or light soils) or spring (colder districts and heavy or wet soils). Transplant either the whole batch or pairs of plants to leave every third one *in situ*: which method you choose is not as important as ensuring sufficient room for unimpeded growth.

MORE WAYS TO RAISE PLANTS

Buying plants and sowing seeds are the two main ways to introduce new plants. If you want to multiply flowers already growing in the garden – to expand your plantings,

ways to take cuttings, but the types most useful for garden flowers are stem tip, basal and root cuttings.

Stem tip cuttings

These are the upper portions of strong healthy shoots without flowers or flower buds, taken any time during the growing season.

Using a sharp knife or secateurs, cut off about 10cm (4in) of stem tip, trim the base just below a leaf joint or 'node' and strip the leaves from the bottom third of the cutting. Insert this bared section in a pot of cuttings compost (several will fit readily into a 15cm/6in pot without touching each other), firm gently with your fingers and water with a fine rose.

To keep humidity at the right level, stand the pot in a propagator or cover with a plastic bag supported clear of the foliage on canes or wire hoops. Keep in a warm place in good light, shaded from hot sun; keep consistently moist. After two to four weeks fresh young growth or roots appearing at the pot base will indicate successful rooting, and the cuttings can then be transferred to individual 8–10cm (3–4in) pots in cooler surroundings.

Some of the flowers commonly propagated in this way are arctotis, dianthus, erysimum, fuchsia, gazania, oenothera, pelargonium and penstemon.

Basal cuttings

This variation of the stem tip method uses short young shoots 5–8cm (2–3in) high appearing on dormant crowns in spring. Follow the same procedure but make sure you include a small piece of the woody basal tissue at the bottom of each stem, and dip each cutting in hormone rooting powder before setting it in the compost. Flowers that respond well to this technique include anthemis, chrysanthemum, dahlia, delphinium, lupin and monarda.

Examples of the flower kingdom's more eccentric characters: dicentra or bleeding heart (left), a shade-loving gem for a sheltered spot under deciduous trees, and the thimble-shaped heads of sun-loving eryngium or sea holly (right), with each electric blue flower sitting on a spiny ruff like an exploding star. Both deserve prominence among plainer neighbours.

Root cuttings

This is an easy and reliable way to produce large numbers of new plants from healthy perennials while they are still dormant in winter, and the only way to multiply border phlox free from the risk of eelworm infection (but note that variegated phlox cultivars produce all-green plants by this method).

Lift smaller donor plants out of the ground with a fork, and wash or shake off some of the soil; with larger specimens scrape away the soil to expose enough roots. Look for three to four fat, healthy, pliable roots and cut these off close to their origin; then replant or re-cover donors straight away.

Trim the thick roots of plants like acanthus or anchusa into 5–8cm (2–3in) sections, making a straight cut at the top end – that nearest the crown of the original plant – and a slanting cut at the other. Insert cuttings vertically about 5cm (2in) apart in a pot of cuttings compost, with the top (straight) end at surface level. Firm in, cover with a 1cm (½in) layer of grit, and water in.

Thinner roots (campanula, phlox, *Primula denticulata*,

for example) are simply trimmed to length and laid horizontally on the surface of a box of compost, covered with a 5cm (2in) depth of compost and the top dressing of grit. Keep all root cuttings in a propagator or cold frame until young shoots develop and fresh roots appear at the base, when they may be potted up individually.

Other suitable subjects for root cuttings include dicentra, echinops, eryngium, gypsophila, macleaya, mertensia, oriental poppies, pulsatilla, romneya, stokesia, trollius and verbascum.

HARDENING OFF

This is a vital transition stage that acclimatizes young plants raised indoors from seeds or cuttings to the

Layering

Many perennials that sprawl, trail or run at ground level spread by rooting their long shoots wherever they touch the ground – creeping Jenny, border carnations, periwinkles, *Persicaria affinis* and wild strawberry, for example. Simply sever any rooted layers and transplant them elsewhere, or peg down young shoots in the soil or pots of moist compost until they form roots or plantlets, when they can safely be detached.

Named dahlias such as the perennially popular 'Bishop of Llandaff' are propagated from cuttings or tuber divisions to ensure true to type offspring. Seeds produce variable plants; the unpredictable process has resulted in the carefully refined 'Bishop's Children' mixture.

rigours of the world outside. Whether they are hardy or half-hardy, abruptly exposing them to cold winds or low temperatures will at best check growth for a while, but could even prove lethal to their soft unprepared tissues.Do not plant out any half-hardy flowers until all risk of frost is past, but start preparing them about three weeks before the last average frost date.

If you have a cool greenhouse or conservatory, move plants there for a few days and then transfer them to a cold frame, keeping this closed and covered with sacking or old carpet in the event of frost. Gradually admit a little air to the frame until eventually it is left uncovered, at first only by day but later all the time unless the weather turns very cold.

Alternatively just stand plants in a sheltered place outdoors on mild days, bringing them in again at night. Gradually expose them for longer by day and then at night as well. After about two to three weeks they should be ready to plant out.

Saving your own seeds

Many flowers self-seed lavishly, especially sweet Alison, calendula, foxgloves, nigella, nasturtiums and verbascums. The resulting seedlings can be left where they choose to grow for a random cottage-garden effect or may be transplanted elsewhere when large enough to handle. Deliberately saving your own seeds is economical and a valuable way to perpetuate many choice varieties, especially novel mutations or 'sports' (highly bred cultivars may produce some surprises, not always welcome). Select the best donors, leave their seed heads until almost ripe and gather them in paper bags before they can shed their contents. When quite dry, clean out the seeds and store them in paper envelopes labelled with name, date and site, in a cool dry place until it is time to sow them.

4

CARING
for
FLOWERS

Compared with some other kinds of plants –
vegetables, houseplants or high alpines, for
example – garden flowers are seldom difficult to
tend, and many almost look after themselves.
Some old-fashioned flower varieties exist today
only because they have managed to survive years
of neglect in some forgotten corner. Provided you
give your plants a good start in life, a simple
programme of basic care is often sufficient to
ensure a glorious, ever-changing display to light
up your garden for months or years ahead.

Special needs

Some kinds of flowers need exceptional care with soil preparation.

- Most alpines and rock plants detest lingering moisture at surface level, so make sure drainage is efficient (or build a special raised bed instead), add plenty of grit to planting sites and mulch all round plants with 2.5–5cm (1–2in) of grit or shingle.
- When planting bulbs in heavy clay soils, ensure free drainage by adding coarse sand or grit to the plantng sites, and bed especially sensitive kinds like lilies on their sides on a 5cm (2in) layer of grit.
- Wildflowers have usually evolved in unmanaged, even impoverished habitats and will grow and flower best without any preliminary manuring or subsequent feeding.
- Marginal and bog plants enjoy wet soils, which do not need further amendment beyond forking over; mulch with garden compost or composted bark rather than manure near water features to avoid nutrients leaching and feeding algae.

PREPARING TO PLANT

Investing a little care right at the outset to help plants settle comfortably and promptly into their new homes can reap dividends for long afterwards. A few might have special requirements, but the majority are content with a well-broken, weed-free site with adequate drainage and plenty of humus, which is partially decayed organic matter that improves all soils, supplies plant foods and gives life and colour to the topsoil, where your plants root most extensively.

New or neglected ground may need thorough digging to break up compacted areas, improve drainage and aeration, and allow you to remove perennial weeds, which could prove difficult to extract later without a lot of disturbance. Try to remove as many root fragments as possible of persistent weeds like ground elder and couch grass. When you feel the ground is reasonably clean, fork in a generous amount of garden compost, well-rotted manure (at least two years old), leafmould or composted (not freshly shredded) bark. If supplies are rationed, concentrate these soil improvers in specific planting sites rather than distributing them throughout.

This initial work may seem onerous – if so, divide areas into manageable stages and take regular breaks – but should need doing only once: an annual spring mulch of organic material or a sprinkle of slow-release fertilizer (see pages 95–7) should maintain the improvement thereafter.

Many soils do not require digging, but will become crumbly in texture after just superficial loosening with a fork. However, all benefit from enrichment with humus. Remember that trying to change, rather than improve, the nature of your soil is often futile, and that suitable flowers exist for almost every 'difficult' soil type (see pages 56–9).

PLANTING

The day before you plant, use a rake to loosen the surface and stir in a dressing of general fertilizer (see page 95). Just before planting, assemble all the plants, water them well and leave for an hour or two to drain.

If you are planting up a large area, set the plants out on the soil first to make sure you are satisfied with the arrangement, but do not leave bare-root plants exposed for long to wind or hot sun. On heavy or moist soil stand on a plank to distribute your weight and protect the surface.

1. Dig individual holes for large plants with a spade; use a trowel for smaller plants, holding it as you would a dagger to chop out the holes.
2. Test each hole to see that it has enough room for the plant to fit comfortably at the same depth as it was growing before.
3. Centre the plant, holding it upright, and backfill all round the roots with loose soil; firm in place with both hands, and water thoroughly.

Match plants with the soil they prefer or amend the planting area to suit. Goat's rue (*Galega officinalis*), for example, (page 88) is an easy-going cottage garden perennial enjoying the same light and soil conditions as roses, whereas fritillaries such as crown imperials (above) need very well-drained ground, so plant their bulbs on their sides on a bed of grit in heavier soil.

With bare-rooted plants take a little extra care to spread out the roots evenly, and then work some of the soil between them as you backfill. When planting bulbs use a trowel or cylindrical bulb planter to open up a flat-bottomed hole deep enough to cover the bulb with twice its own depth of soil. Drifts of bulbs can be planted together at the bottom of wider holes dug with a spade.

When to plant

If possible, always plant when the soil is moist, during a showery spell or just before rain is forecast. Container-grown plants can be introduced almost any time the ground is workable and not frozen or waterlogged, but you may need to tend late spring and summer newcomers more attentively in a hot or dry season.

For peace of mind, follow these ideal timings.

- Half-hardy plants – after the last spring frosts; protect or bring indoors before the first autumn frost.
- Hardy biennials – early to mid-autumn, or early spring in cold districts.
- Hardy perennials – bare-rooted kinds while they are dormant, preferably during mid- to late autumn on free-draining ground or early spring on cold heavy soils; container-grown plants during autumn or spring.
- Bulbs – winter and spring-flowering kinds by late autumn (narcissi by the end of late summer, most others in early autumn, tulips late autumn); summer

---

'Knocking out' plants

When removing a plant from its container you may be able to free it by tapping the edge of the pot sharply on a spade handle or by smacking the base with the palm of your hand. Tight plastic pots can be cut open with scissors; ease a stubborn rootball from a clay pot by sliding a spatula or knife round its circumference. Remove bedding plants from trays with a trowel or slide out the entire contents and separate plants with your fingers.

---

bulbs (galtonias, gladioli, sparaxis, for example) in early spring, autumn bulbs (colchicums, nerines, sternbergia) up to mid-summer.

MULCHING

Covering the soil with a protective mulch delays evaporation and thus reduces the need for watering, shields the surface from the effects of extreme weather, suppresses annual weeds and, if you use an organic material, helps maintain soil structure and fertility. Mulching is generally (but not exclusively) used for perennials rather than annuals or bedding plants.

Materials to use include well-rotted manure, garden compost, leafmould, shredded bark, grass clippings (no

A mulch can benefit gardens and gardeners alike. Around plants an organic mulch stabilizes and improves the ground, protecting even durable border favourites like phlox and acanthus (below) from extreme conditions. On paths it is a complementary and labour-saving finish.

Astrantia or masterwort is an old-fashioned cottage garden perennial with papery bracts suggestive of sun-loving 'everlasting' flowers, but in fact it has a deep preference for partial shade and moist soils or regular watering in dry weather.

deeper than 2.5cm/1in at each dressing) and mushroom compost (not for acid-loving plants). Inorganic mulches like gravel, slate, glass beads and crushed metal fragments can enhance containers and specimen plantings, and protect the soil without improving its character. Grit is used for damp-sensitive plants such as alpines and also as an efficient slug deterrent.

Since a mulch will delay changes to the soil, apply in late spring when the ground is moist and warming up, spreading an even layer 5–8cm (2–3in) deep, and top up annually.

WATERING

Fortifying the soil with plenty of humus and then insulating the surface with a generous mulch can postpone or even cancel the need to water flowers in the ground. But in a prolonged dry or unusually hot season soil reserves of moisture are eventually depleted, and watering becomes essential before plants begin to suffer and wilt. The cue for action is when soil as deep as 5cm (2in) below the surface is dry.

Concentrate on the plants most at risk: those recently introduced or moved for about six weeks after planting, seedlings and young plants, all those growing in containers and all moisture-loving kinds. Identify plants which tolerate drought well – established perennials such as acanthus, euphorbia, kniphofia, salvia and sedum, for example, and annuals like arctotis, cosmos, nasturtium, tagetes and zinnia – and leave these until last if water or time is short.

Collect and save rainwater in butts and other storage containers, and always use a watering can to target individual plants precisely. Give each a good soak every week in dry weather, and add or top up mulching material afterwards to trap the moisture. Water in the evening or early morning. Large beds and borders can be supplied with porous or perforated 'seep' or 'leaky' hoses, laid in parallel under a mulch and connected to a mains tap (although the use of these may be banned wherever a drought order is in force).

FEEDING

In many gardens perennials survive for years without feeding, and annuals perform well with perhaps an occasional liquid feed, but all (except wild species) flower more profusely if soil fertility is kept topped up, especially where exhausted top growth is cleared at the end of the season and not returned later as garden compost.

Preparing the soil thoroughly before planting (see pages 90–91) and finishing with an organic mulch (page 92) can supply most needs. When planting rake in a top-dressing of fertilizer such as pelleted poultry manure (for rapid response) or blood, fish and bone (for slow-release nutrients).

Lavish planting in a hanging basket can look stunning but makes huge demands on a limited compost supply. Water daily in hot weather; reduce moisture loss with a saucer in the bottom of the basket and water-retaining crystals in the compost.

Close planting in mutually supportive communities can relieve you of the
need to stake and tie plants. Japanese anemones (foreground below), for
example, may reach 1.5m (5ft) or more in good soil, and can be vulnerable
to strong winds without a little help from their neighbours.

Supplementary food should then be unnecessary, except for container plants, which need regular feeding from about six weeks after planting, when compost nutrients are usually depleted. With the possibility of milder autumns as climate change progresses, one or two high-potash feeds after mid-summer could prolong displays late into the season. Flowers like dahlias, chrysanthemums and sweet peas grown for show have their own intensive feeding regimes.

SUPPORT

One sign of over-feeding is soft weak growth that cannot support itself. Some plants are naturally less sturdy than others and tend to flop at or just after flowering time – border phlox, *Gaura lindheimeri*, heleniums and herbaceous geraniums, for example – and very tall flowers like delphiniums, eremurus, hollyhocks and sunflowers easily fall victim to winds. Once plants collapse they are difficult to salvage.

Avoid a dishevelled garden by growing weaker plants among more robust neighbours (choose shorter or even dwarf cultivars in exposed gardens), and by buttressing vulnerable plants well before they need it. A variety of supports can be used, from canes, stakes, hazel poles or spiral metal rods for tall specimens, to linked wire stakes or twiggy prunings for bushy, thin-stemmed clumps. If installed well in advance, supports are often

Autumn versus spring cleaning

Flower gardens have traditionally been tidied in autumn, with every dead leaf and stem conscientiously cleared out of sight, but delaying this familiar ritual until late winter or early spring can have benefits. Dead standing growth will help protect dormant crowns from cold weather and offer shelter for hibernating insect allies such as lacewings and ladybirds. In spring the dead material often crumbles into a useful instant mulch, returning valuable nutrients to the soil. And standing stems embroidered with frost crystals or beads of mist are among winter's unexpected delights.

disguised by subsequent growth.

Supply climbers like *Cobaea scandens* and sweet peas with a strong framework such as tripods of bamboo canes, wicker pyramids, trellis, netting or wall wires, and if necessary tie in wayward growth as it advances. Weaker climbers like eccremocarpus and border clematis (*C. integrifolia* and *C. recta*) are best sited where they can scramble over low shrubs and stouter neighbours.

Lady's mantle (*Alchemilla mollis*) is a valuable and hard-working perennial with sprays of tiny yellow-green flowers in summer and handsome lobed leaves that glisten with drops after rain. Cutting clumps almost to ground level after flowering refreshes the foliage and forestalls liberal self-seeding.

GROOMING

Cutting off blooms as they fade (deadheading) helps maintain an orderly appearance in a bed or border, conserves a plant's energy and will often extend the flowering display or even stimulate plants like catmint, lupins, delphiniums and sages to produce a second (though smaller) flush later in the year.

Do not deadhead any plants intended to supply seeds or provide decorative seedheads – for example, baptisia, eryngiums, honesty, *Iris foetidissima*, nectaroscordum and many alliums, and numerous ornamental grasses. Deadheading annuals will usually prolong flowering, although many varieties are 'self-cleaning' and shed faded blooms unaided.

Spring- and early-summer-flowering perennials often become straggly and untidy after their display, and benefit from shearing to ground level to encourage fresh, more attractive foliage. As the growing season closes, many hardy perennials die back to ground level; remove and discard any dead foliage that showed signs of disease, and also tidy plants like hostas whose lush leaves can become a soggy haven for slugs and snails. Whether you also clear the dead growth from other flowers in autumn depends on your standards of tidiness (see box on page 97).

With their huge rosettes of grey felted leaves and towering spires of flowers, mulleins (*Verbascum*) qualify equally for supporting roles at the back of displays and as solo stars in prominent positions. Flowering continues on numerous sideshoots if main spikes are removed when their blooms fade.

Aristocrats of the late summer flower garden, white or blue agapanthus are often confined to large containers, where their marginally frost-sensitive crowns can be tucked up with a protective mulch in a cold winter.

ENSURING GOOD HEALTH

Like every living organism, flowering plants are susceptible in varying degrees to disorders, but it is easy to become over-sensitive to the threat from pests and diseases. Some are cosmetic, specific, uncommon or apparently tolerated by plants; others have natural controls such as predators that may be encouraged by wildlife-friendly management; and many problems appear as a result of mistaken gardening habits.

To ensure relative freedom from trouble:

- Choose flowers appropriate to your soil, aspect, exposure and local climate.
- Select naturally robust or resilient varieties of disease-prone plants – rust-resistant antirrhinums and hollyhocks, for example.
- Diversify plants in a mixed community, where they are less vulnerable than in a monoculture (a mass planting of the same species).
- Avoid unnecessary stress to plants by providing adequate water, food and protection before their need is urgent and results in disorders.
- Control weeds, which may be alternative hosts for problems, and threatening competition from neighbouring plants.
- Inspect plants regularly for early signs of trouble,

identify the cause and respond with simple targeted measures like pruning and destroying diseased foliage or blasting off aphids with a pressure sprayer.

- Avoid chemical remedies, many of which also kill beneficial organisms or eventually generate immunity.
- If the problem persists, cull the victim and either try again elsewhere or grow an unrelated substitute.

THE END OF THE SEASON

As temperatures fall, day length shortens and growth comes to a temporary standstill, check that all is in order in the flower garden.

Half-hardy plants need propagating or housing under cover before frosts set in, and borderline plants like agapanthus, penstemons and *Verbena bonariensis* may need protecting where they grow with a thick blanket of dry material such as leaves, bracken or conifer prunings.

Insulate containers of perennials with sacking, fleece or 'bubble' polythene and move them to a sheltered spot. Bring pots and hanging baskets under glass to allow half-hardy bedding to continue flowering a little longer in frost-free conditions. Collect any ripe seeds for drying and storing or for sowing immediately if appropriate, and take cuttings while growth is still firm and undamaged.

Then reflect on the past performance of your plants and start planning any changes or developments, especially where this involves sowing new seeds and

Winter colour

Depending on locality and the severity of the weather, you could have a variety of plants flowering in your garden during the short days of winter, among them precocious species and cultivars such as *Adonis amurensis* and *A. vernalis*, *Anemone blanda*, crocuses like *C.* 'Golden Bunch' and *C. tommasinianus*, *Cyclamen coum*, *Eranthis hyemalis*, *Galanthus elwesii*, hellebores – especially *Helleborus argutifolius* and *H. niger*, *Iris reticulata* and *I. unguicularis*, *Narcissus asturiensis* and *N. cyclamineus* species and hybrids, *Primula vulgaris* subsp. *sibthorpii*, *Pulmonaria rubra*, saxifrages like *S. burseriana*, *Scilla mischtschenkoana* and *Tulipa humilis*.

Combine these in generous patches with foliage plants and grasses like ajuga, arum, bergenia, carex, *Euphorbia characias*, *Iris foetidissima*, ophiopogon, *Sedum spathulifolium*, sempervivums and stipa for colourful compositions that will herald the end of winter and an encouraging start to a new season in the flower garden.

ordering or moving plants. Although most flowers are dying down and becoming dormant, others are already stirring into life below ground. A flower garden rarely sleeps for long in winter.

INDEX

Page numbers in *italics* refer to captions to the illustrations